Items should be returned on or before the last date shown below. Items not already requested by other borrowers may be renewed in person, in writing or by telephone. To renew, please quote the number on the barcode label. To renew online a PIN is required. This can be requested at your local library.
Renew online @ **www.dublincitypubliclibraries.ie**
Fines charged for overdue items will include postage incurred in recovery. Damage to or loss of items will be charged to the borrower.

**Leabharlanna Poiblí Chathair Bhaile Átha Cliath**
**Dublin City Public Libraries**

Baile Átha Cliath
Dublin City

D0280065

| Date Due | Date Due | Date Due |
| --- | --- | --- |
| | | |

No one
characteristic
clasps us purely
and universally
in its embrace.'

MICHEL DE MONTAIGNE
Born 1533, Aquitaine, France
Died 1592, Aquitaine, France

Montaigne wrote and revised his *Essays*
between 1570 and 1592.

MONTAIGNE IN PENGUIN CLASSICS
*The Complete Essays*
*An Apology for Raymond Sebond*
*On Friendship*
*On Solitude*
*The Essays: A Selection*

# MICHEL DE MONTAIGNE

*How We Weep and Laugh
at the Same Thing*

*Translated by*
M. A. Screech

PENGUIN BOOKS

PENGUIN CLASSICS

Published by the Penguin Group
Penguin Books Ltd, 80 Strand, London WC2R 0RL, England
Penguin Group (USA) Inc., 375 Hudson Street, New York, New York 10014, USA
Penguin Group (Canada), 90 Eglinton Avenue East, Suite 700, Toronto, Ontario,
Canada M4P 2Y3 (a division of Pearson Penguin Canada Inc.)
Penguin Ireland, 25 St Stephen's Green, Dublin 2, Ireland
(a division of Penguin Books Ltd)
Penguin Group (Australia), 707 Collins Street, Melbourne, Victoria 3008, Australia
(a division of Pearson Australia Group Pty Ltd)
Penguin Books India Pvt Ltd, 11 Community Centre, Panchsheel Park,
New Delhi – 110 017, India
Penguin Group (NZ), 67 Apollo Drive, Rosedale, Auckland 0632, New Zealand
(a division of Pearson New Zealand Ltd)
Penguin Books (South Africa) (Pty) Ltd, Block D, Rosebank Office Park,
181 Jan Smuts Avenue, Parktown North, Gauteng 2193, South Africa

Penguin Books Ltd, Registered Offices: 80 Strand, London WC2R 0RL, England

www.penguin.com

This edition published in Penguin Classics 2015
002

Translation and editorial material copyright © M. A. Screech, 1987, 1991, 2003

Set in 9.5/13 pt Baskerville 10 Pro
Typeset by Jouve (UK), Milton Keynes
Printed in Great Britain by Clays Ltd, St Ives plc

A CIP catalogue record for this book is available from the British Library

ISBN: 978-0-141-39722-1

www.greenpenguin.co.uk

# *Contents*

# *How We Weep and Laugh at the Same Thing*

*[ An understanding of the complexity of conflicting emotions helps us to avoid trivial interpretations of great men and their grief.]*

When we read in our history books that Antigonus was severely displeased with his son for having brought him the head of his enemy King Pyrrhus who had just been killed fighting against him and that he burst into copious tears when he saw it; and that Duke René of Lorraine also lamented the death of Duke Charles of Burgundy whom he had just defeated, and wore mourning at his funeral; and that at the battle of Auroy which the Count de Montfort won against Charles de Blois, his rival for the Duchy of Brittany, the victor showed great grief when he happened upon his enemy's corpse: we should not at once exclaim,

> *Et cosi aven che l'animo ciascuna*
> *Sua passion sotto et contrario manto*
> *Ricopre, con la vista hor' chiara hor bruna.*

[Thus does the mind cloak every passion with its opposite, our faces showing now joy, now sadness.]

When they presented Caesar with the head of Pompey our histories say that he turned his gaze away as from a spectacle both ugly and displeasing. There had been such a long understanding and fellowship between them in the management of affairs of State, they had shared the same fortunes and rendered each other so many mutual services as allies, that we should not believe that his behaviour was quite false and counterfeit – as this other poet thinks it was:

> *tutumque putavit*
> *Jam bonus esse socer; lachrimas non sponte cadentes*
> *Effudit, gemitusque expressit pectore læto.*

[And now he thought it was safe to play the good father-in-law; he poured out tears, but not spontaneous ones, and he forced out groans from his happy breast.]

For while it is true that most of our actions are but mask and cosmetic, and that it is sometimes true that

> *Hæredis fletus sub persona risus est;*

[Behind the mask, the tears of an heir are laughter;]

nevertheless we ought to consider when judging such events how our souls are often shaken by conflicting emotions. Even as there is said to be a variety of humours assembled in our bodies, the dominant one being that which normally prevails according to our complexion, so too in our souls: although diverse emotions may shake them, there is one which must remain in possession of the field; nevertheless its victory is not so complete but that the weaker ones do not sometimes regain lost ground because of the pliancy and mutability of our soul and make a brief sally in their turn. That is why we can see that not only children, who artlessly follow Nature, often weep and laugh at the same thing, but that not one of us either can boast that, no matter how much he may want to set out on a journey, he still does not feel his heart a-tremble when he says goodbye to family and friends: even if he does not actually burst into tears at least he puts foot to stirrup with a sad and gloomy face. And however noble the passion which enflames the heart of a well-born bride, she still has to have her arms prised from her mother's neck before being given to her husband, no matter what that merry fellow may say:

> *Est ne novis nuptis odio venus, anne parentum*
> *Frustrantur falsis gaudia lachrimulis,*
> *Ubertim thalami quas intra limina fundunt?*
> *Non, ita me divi, vera gemunt, juverint.*

[Is Venus really hated by our brides, or do they mock their parents' joy with those false tears which they pour forth in abundance at their chamber-door? No. So help me, gods, their sobs are false ones.]

3

And so it is not odd to lament the death of a man whom we would by no means wish to be still alive.

When I rail at my manservant I do so sincerely with all my mind: my curses are real not feigned. But once I cease to fume, if he needs help from me I am glad to help him: I turn over the page. When I call him a dolt or a calf I have no intention of stitching such labels on to him for ever: nor do I believe I am contradicting myself when I later call him an honest fellow. No one characteristic clasps us purely and universally in its embrace. If only talking to oneself did not look mad, no day would go by without my being heard growling to myself, against myself, 'You silly shit!' Yet I do not intend that to be a definition of me.

If anyone should think when he sees me sometimes look bleakly at my wife and sometimes lovingly that either emotion is put on, then he is daft. When Nero took leave of his mother whom he was sending to be drowned, he nevertheless felt some emotion at his mother's departure and felt horror and pity.

The sun, they say, does not shed its light in one continuous flow but ceaselessly darts fresh rays so thickly at us, one after another, that we cannot perceive any gap between them:

> *Largus enim liquidi fons luminis, ætherius sol*
> *Inrigat assidue cœlum candore recenti,*
> *Suppeditatque novo confestim lumine lumen.*

[That generous source of liquid light, the aethereal sun, assiduously floods the heavens with new rays and ceaselessly sheds light upon new light.]

So, too, our soul darts its arrows separately but imperceptibly.

Artabanus happened to take his nephew Xerxes by surprise. He teased him about the sudden change which he saw come over his face. But Xerxes was in fact thinking about the huge size of his army as it was crossing the Hellespont for the expedition against Greece; he first felt a quiver of joy at seeing so many thousands of men devoted to his service and showed this by a happy and festive look on his face; then, all of a sudden his thoughts turned to all those lives which would wither in a hundred years at most: he knit his brow and was saddened to tears.

We have pursued revenge for an injury with a resolute will; we have felt a singular joy at our victory . . . and we weep: yet it is not for that that we weep. Nothing has changed; but our mind contemplates the matter in a different light and sees it from another aspect: for everything has many angles and many different sheens. Thoughts of kinship, old acquaintanceships and affections suddenly seize our minds and stir them each according to their worth: but the change is so sudden that it escapes us:

> *Nil adeo fieri celeri ratione videtur*
> *Quam si mens fieri proponit et inchoat ipsa.*

> *Ocius ergo animus quam res se perciet ulla,*
> *Ante oculos quarum in promptu natura videtur.*

[Nothing can be seen to match the rapidity of the thoughts which the mind produces and initiates. The mind is swifter than anything which the nature of our eyes allows them to see.]

That is why we deceive ourselves if we want to make this never-ending succession into one continuous whole. When Timoleon weeps for the murder which, with noble determination, he committed, he does not weep for the liberty he has restored to his country; he does not weep for the Tyrant: he weeps for his brother. He has done one part of his duty: let us allow him to do the other.

# On conscience

*[Conscience originally meant connivance. Conscience in the sense of our individual consciousness of right and wrong or of our own guilt or rectitude fascinated Montaigne. It became a vital concern of his during the Wars of Religion with their cruelties, their false accusations and their use of torture on prisoners. Such moral basis as there was for the 'question' (judicial torture) seems, curiously enough, to have been a respect for the power of conscience − of a man's inner sense of his guilt or innocence which would strengthen or weaken his power to withstand pain. A major source of Montaigne's ideas here is St Augustine and a passionate note by Juan Luis Vives in his edition of the* City of God *designed to undermine confidence in torture.]*

During our civil wars I was travelling one day with my brother the Sieur de la Brousse when we met a gentleman of good appearance who was on the other side from us; I did not know anything about that since he feigned otherwise. The worst of these wars is that the cards are so mixed up, with your enemy indistinguishable from you by any clear indication of language or deportment, being brought up under the same laws, manners and climate, that it is not easy to avoid confusion and disorder. That made me fear that I myself would come upon our own troops in a place where I was not known, be obliged to state my name and wait for the worst. That did happen to me on another occasion: for, from just such a mishap, I lost men and horses. Among others, they killed one of my pages, pitifully: an Italian of good family whom I was carefully training; in him was extinguished a young life, beautiful and full of great promise.

But that man of mine was so madly afraid! I noticed that he nearly died every time we met any horsemen or passed through towns loyal to the King; I finally guessed that his alarm arose from his conscience. It seemed to that wretched man that you could read right into the very secret thoughts of his mind through his mask and the crosses on his greatcoat. So wondrous is the power of conscience! It makes us betray, accuse and fight against ourselves. In default of an outside testimony it leads us to witness against ourselves:

*Occultum quatiens animo tortore flagellum.*

[Lashing us with invisible whips, our soul torments us.]

The following story is on the lips of children: a Paeon-ian called Bessus was rebuked for having deliberately destroyed a nest of swallows, killing them all. He said he was right to do so: those little birds kept falsely accusing him of having murdered his father! Until then this act of parricide had been hidden and unknown; but the avenging Furies of his conscience made him who was to pay the penalty reveal the crime.

Hesiod corrects that saying of Plato's, that the punishment follows hard upon the sin. He says it is born at the same instant, with the sin itself; to expect punishment is to suffer it: to merit it is to expect it. Wickedness forges torments for itself,

> *Malum consilium consultori pessimum,*

> [Who counsels evil, suffers evil most,]

just as the wasp harms others when it stings but especially itself, for it loses sting and strength for ever:

> *Vitasque in vulnere ponunt.*

> [In that wound they lay down their lives.]

The Spanish blister-fly secretes an antidote to its poison, by some mutual antipathy within nature. So too, just when we take pleasure in vice, there is born in our conscience an opposite displeasure, which tortures us, sleeping and waking, with many painful thoughts.

> *Quippe ubi se multi, per somnia sæpe loquentes,*
> *Aut morbo delirantes, procraxe ferantur,*
> *Et celata diu in medium peccala dedisse.*

[Many indeed, often talking in their sleep or delirious in illness, have proclaimed, it is said, and betrayed long-hidden sins.]

Apollodorus dreamed that he saw himself being flayed by the Scythians then boiled in a pot while his heart kept muttering, 'I am the cause of all these ills.' No hiding-place awaits the wicked, said Epicurus, for they can never be certain of hiding there while their conscience gives them away.

> *Prima est hæc ultio, quod se*
> *Judice nemo nocens absolvitur.*

[This is the principal vengeance: no guilty man is absolved: he is his own judge.]

Conscience can fill us with fear, but she can also fill us with assurance and confidence. And I can say that I have walked more firmly through some dangers by reflecting on the secret knowledge I had of my own will and the innocence of my designs.

> *Conscia mens ut cuique sua est, ita concipit intra*
> *Pectora pro facto spemque metumque suo.*

[A mind conscious of what we have done conceives within our breast either hope or fear, according to our deeds.]

There are hundreds of examples: it will suffice to cite three of them about the same great man.

When Scipio was arraigned one day before the Roman

people on a grave indictment, instead of defending himself and flattering his judges he said: 'Your wishing to judge, on a capital charge, a man through whom you have authority to judge the Roman world, becomes you well!'

Another time his only reply to the accusations made against him by a Tribune of the People was not to plead his cause but to say: 'Come, fellow citizens! Let us go and give thanks to the gods for the victory they gave me over the Carthaginians on just such a day as this!' Then as he started to walk towards the temple all the assembled people could be seen following after him – even his prosecutor.

Again when Petilius, under the instigation of Cato, demanded that Scipio account for the monies that had passed through his hands in the province of Antioch, Scipio came to the Senate for this purpose, took his account-book from under his toga and declared that it contained the truth about his receipts and expenditure; but when he was told to produce it as evidence he refused to do so, saying that he had no wish to act so shamefully towards himself; in the presence of the Senate he tore it up with his own hands. I do not believe that a soul with seared scars could have counterfeited such assurance. He had, says Livy, a mind too great by nature, a mind too elevated by Fortune, even to know how to be a criminal or to condescend to the baseness of defending his innocence.

Torture is a dangerous innovation; it would appear that

it is an assay not of the truth but of a man's endurance. The man who can endure it hides the truth: so does he who cannot. For why should pain make me confess what is true rather than force me to say what is not true? And on the contrary if a man who has not done what he is accused of is able to support such torment, why should a man who has done it be unable to support it, when so beautiful a reward as life itself is offered him?

I think that this innovation is founded on the importance of the power of conscience. It would seem that in the case of the guilty man it would weaken him and assist the torture in making him confess his fault, whereas it strengthens the innocent man against the torture. But to speak the truth, it is a method full of danger and uncertainty. What would you *not* say, what would you *not* do, to avoid such grievous pain?

*Etiam innocentes cogit mentiri dolor.*

[Pain compels even the innocent to lie.]

This results in a man whom the judge has put to the torture lest he die innocent being condemned to die both innocent and tortured. Thousands upon thousands have falsely confessed to capital charges. Among them, after considering the details of the trial which Alexander made him face and the way he was tortured, I place Philotas.

All the same it is , so they say, the least bad method that human frailty has been able to discover. Very inhumanely, however, and very ineffectually in my opinion. Many peoples less barbarous in this respect than the Greeks and the Romans who call them the Barbarians reckon it horrifying and cruel to torture and smash a man of whose crime you are still in doubt. That ignorant doubt is yours: what has it to do with him? You are the unjust one, are you not? who do worse than kill a man so as not to kill him without due cause! You can prove that by seeing how frequently a man prefers to die for no reason at all rather than to pass through such a questioning which is more painful than the death-penalty itself and which by its harshness often anticipates that penalty by carrying it out.

I do not know where I heard this from, but it exactly represents the conscience of our own Justice: a village woman accused a soldier before his commanding general – a great man for justice – of having wrenched from her little children such sops as she had left to feed them with, the army having laid waste all the surrounding villages. As for proof, there was none. That general first summoned the woman to think carefully what she was saying, especially since she would be guilty of perjury if she were lying; she persisted, so he had the soldier's belly slit open in order to throw the light of truth on to the fact. The woman was found to be right. An investigatory condemnation!

# Fortune is often found in Reason's train

[*The Roman censor was not too happy about Montaigne's writing about Fortune (as distinct from Providence) – strangely so, since fickle Fortune and Fortune's Wheel were centuries-old commonplaces. (The word* Fortune *itself occurs some 350 times in the* Essays.*)*]

The changeableness of Fortune's varied dance means that she must inevitably show us every kind of face. Has any of her actions ever been more expressly just than the following? The Duke of Valentinois decided to poison Adrian the Cardinal of Corneto, to whose home in the Vatican he and his father Pope Alexander VI were coming to dine; so he sent ahead a bottle of poisoned wine with instructions to the butler to look after it carefully. The Pope, chancing to arrive before his son, asked for a drink; that butler, who thought that the wine had been entrusted to him merely because of its quality, served it to him; then the Duke himself, arriving just in time for dinner and trusting that nobody would have touched his bottle, drank some too, so that the father died suddenly while the son, after being tormented by a long illness, was reserved for a worse and different fortune.

Sometimes it seems that Fortune is literally playing with us. The Seigneur d'Estrées (who was then ensign to Monseigneur de Vendôme) and the Seigneur de Licques (a lieutenant in the forces of the Duke of Aerschot) were both suitors of the sister of the Sieur de Fouquerolle – despite their being on opposite sides, as often happens with neighbours on the frontier. The Seigneur de Licques was successful. However, on his very wedding-day and, what is worse, before going to bed, the bridegroom desired to break a lance as a tribute to his new bride and went out skirmishing near St Omer; there, he was taken prisoner by the Seigneur d'Estrées who had proved the stronger. To exploit this advantage to the full, d'Estrées compelled the lady –

> *Conjugis ante coacta novi dimittere collum,*
> *Quam veniens una atque altera rursus hyems*
> *Noctibus in longis avidum saturasset amorem.*

[Forced to release her embrace of her young husband before the long nights of a couple of winters had sated her eager love] –

personally to beg him, of his courtesy, to surrender his prisoner to her. Which he did, the French nobility never refusing anything to the ladies . . .

Was the following not Fate apparently playing the artist? The Empire of Constantinople was founded by Constantine son of Helena: many centuries later it was ended by another Constantine son of Helena!

Sometimes it pleases Fortune to rival our Christian miracles. We hold that when King Clovis was besieging Angoulême, by God's favour the walls collapsed of themselves; Bouchet borrows from some other author an account of what happened when King Robert was laying siege to a certain city: he slipped off to Orleans to celebrate the festival of St Aignan; while he was saying his prayers, at a certain point in the Mass the walls of the besieged city collapsed without being attacked. But Fortune produced quite opposite results during our Milanese wars: for after Captain Renzo had mined a great stretch of the wall while besieging the town of Arona for us French it was blown right up in the air, only to fall straight back on to its foundations all in one piece so that the besieged were no worse off.

Sometimes Fortune dabbles in medicine. Jason Phereus was given up by his doctors because of a tumour on the breast; wishing to rid himself of it even by death, he threw himself recklessly into battle where the enemy was thickest; he was struck through the body at precisely the right spot, lancing his tumour and curing him.

Did Fortune not surpass Protogenes the painter in mastery of his art? He had completed a portrait of a tired and exhausted dog; he was pleased with everything else but could not paint its foaming slaver to his own satisfaction; irritated against his work, he grabbed a sponge and threw it at it, intending to blot everything out since the sponge was impregnated with a variety of paints: Fortune guided his throw right to the mouth of the dog and produced the effect which his art had been unable to attain.

Does she not sometimes direct our counsels and correct them? Queen Isabella of England had to cross over to her kingdom from Zealand with her army to come to the aid of her son against her husband; she would have been undone if she had landed at the port she had intended, for her enemies were awaiting her there; but Fortune drove her unwillingly to another place, where she landed in complete safety. And that Ancient who chucked a stone at a dog only to hit his stepmother and kill her could he not have rightly recited this verse:

*Ταντόματον ἡμῶν καλλίω βουλεύεται.*

'Fortune has better counsel than we do.' Icetes had bribed two soldiers to murder Tomoleon during his stay in Adrana in Sicily. They chose a time when he was about to make some sacrifice or other; they mingled with the crowd; just as they were signalling to each other that the time was right for their deed, along comes a third soldier who landed a mighty sword-blow on the head of one of them and then ran away. His companion, believing he was discovered and undone, ran to the altar begging for sanctuary and promising to reveal all the truth. Just as he was giving an account of the conspiracy the third man was caught and was being dragged and manhandled through the crowd towards Timoleon and the more notable members of the congregation: he begged for mercy, saying that he had rightly killed his father's murderer, immediately proving by witnesses which good luck had conveniently provided that his father had indeed been murdered in the town of the Leontines by the very man against whom he had taken his revenge. He was granted ten Attic silver-pounds as a reward for his good luck in saving the life of the Father of the Sicilian People while avenging the death of his own father. Such fortune surpasses in rightness the right-rules of human wisdom.

To conclude. Does not the following reveal a most explicit granting of her favour as well as her goodness and singular piety? The two Ignatii, father and son, having been proscribed by the Roman Triumvirate, nobly decided that their duty was to take each other's life and so frustrate the cruelty of those tyrants. Sword in hand they fell on each other. Fortune guided their sword-points, made both blows equally mortal and honoured the beauty of such a loving affection by giving them just enough strength to withdraw their forearms from the wounds, blood-stained and still grasping their weapons, and to clasp each other, there as they lay, in such an embrace that the executioners cut off both their heads at once, allowing their bodies to remain nobly entwined together, wound against wound, lovingly soaking up each other's life-blood.

# On punishing cowardice

*[Renaissance Jurisconsults such as Tiraquellus were concerned to temper the severity of the Law by examining motives and human limitations. Montaigne does so here in a matter of great concern to gentlemen in time of war.]*

I once heard a prince, a very great general, maintain that a soldier should not be condemned to death for cowardice: he was at table, being told about the trial of the Seigneur de Vervins who was sentenced to death for surrendering Boulogne.

In truth it is reasonable that we should make a great difference between defects due to our weakness and those due to our wickedness. In the latter we deliberately brace ourselves against reason's rules, which are imprinted on us by Nature; in the former it seems we can call Nature herself as a defence-witness for having left us so weak and imperfect. That is why a great many people believe that we can only be punished for deeds done against our conscience: on that rule is partly based the opinion of those who condemn the capital punishment of heretics and misbelievers as well as the opinion that a barrister or a judge cannot be arraigned if they fail in their duty merely from ignorance.

Where cowardice is concerned the usual way is, certainly, to punish it by disgrace and ignominy. It is said that this rule was first introduced by Charondas the lawgiver, and that before his time the laws of Greece condemned to death those who had fled from battle, whereas he ordered that they be made merely to sit for three days in the market-place dressed as women: he hoped he could still make use of them once he had restored their courage by this disgrace – '*Suffundere malis hominis sanguinem quam effundere.*' [Make the blood of a bad man blush not gush.]

It seems too that in ancient times the laws of Rome condemned deserters to death: Ammianus Marcellinus tells how the Emperor Julian condemned ten of his soldiers to be stripped of their rank and then suffer death, 'following,' he said, 'our Ancient laws'. Elsewhere however Julian for a similar fault condemned others to remain among the prisoners under the ensign in charge of the baggage. Even the harsh sentences decreed against those who had fled at Cannae and those who in that same war had followed Gnaeus Fulvius in his defeat did not extend to death.

Yet it is to be feared that disgrace, by making men desperate, may make them not merely estranged but hostile.

When our fathers were young the Seigneur de Franget,

formerly a deputy-commander in the Company of My Lord Marshal de Châtillon, was sent by My Lord Marshal de Chabannes to replace the Seigneur Du Lude as Governor of Fuentarabia; he surrendered it to the Spaniards. He was sentenced to be stripped of his nobility, both he and his descendants being pronounced commoners, liable to taxation and unfit to bear arms. That severe sentence was executed at Lyons. Later all the noblemen who were at Guyse when the Count of Nassau entered it suffered a similar punishment; and subsequently others still.

Anyway, wherever there is a case of ignorance so crass and of cowardice so flagrant as to surpass any norm, that should be an adequate reason for accepting them as proof of wickedness and malice, to be punished as such.

## On the vanity of words

*[Montaigne, despite his own mastery of language, despised words and admired deeds or 'matter'. He showed this before he embarked on the* Essays *in the dedicatory letter of his translation of Raymond Sebond's* Natural Theology, *addressed to his father. What Montaigne admired in ancient Sparta – and what he found lacking in his own day – was a genuine respect for action over rhetoric.]*

In former times there was a rhetorician who said his job was to make trivial things seem big and to be accepted as such. He is a cobbler who can make big shoes fit little feet. In Sparta they would have had him flogged for practising the art of lying and deception. And I am sure that Archidamus their king did not hear without amazement the answer given by Thucydides when he asked him whether he was better at wrestling than Pericles: 'That,' Thucydides replied, 'would be hard to prove: for after I have thrown him to the ground in the match he persuades the spectators that he did not have a fall and is declared the winner.' Those who hide women behind a mask of make-up do less harm, since it is not much of a loss not to see them as they are by nature, whereas rhetoricians pride themselves on deceiving not our eyes but our judgement, bastardizing and corrupting things in their very essence. Countries such as Crete and Sparta which maintained themselves in a sound and regulated polity did not rate orators very highly.

Ariston wisely defined rhetoric as the art of persuading the people; Socrates and Plato, as the art of deceiving and flattering; and those who reject this generic description show it to be true by what they teach. The Mahometans will not allow their children to be taught it because of its uselessness. And the Athenians, despite the fact that the practice of it was esteemed in their city, realizing how pernicious it was, ordained that the main part of it which is to work on the emotions should be abolished, together with formal introductions and perorations.

It is a means invented for manipulating and stirring up the mob and a community fallen into lawlessness; it is a means which, like medicine, is used only when states are sick; in states such as Athens, Rhodes and Rome where the populace, or the ignorant, or all men, held all power and where everything was in perpetual turmoil, the orators flooded in. And in truth few great men in those countries managed to thrust themselves into positions of trust without the help of eloquent speech: Pompey, Caesar, Crassus, Lucullus, Lentulus and Metellus all made it their mainstay for scrambling up towards that grandiose authority which they finally achieved, helped more by rhetoric than by arms, contrary to what was thought right in better times. For Lucius Volumnius, making a public address in favour of the candidates Quintus Fabius and Publius Decius during the consular elections, declared, 'These are great men of action, born for war; they have consular minds, uncouth in verbal conflict. Subtle, eloquent, learned minds are good but for Praetors, administering justice in the City.'

Rhetoric flourished in Rome when their affairs were in their worst state and when they were shattered by the storms of civil war, just as a field left untamed bears the most flourishing weeds.

It would seem that polities which rely on a monarch have less use for it than the others: for that animal-stupidity and levity which are found in the masses, making them apt to be manipulated and swayed through the ears by those sweet harmonious sounds without succeeding in weighing the truth of anything by force of reason – such levity, I repeat, is not so readily found in one individual man; and it is easier to protect him by a good education and counsel from being impressed by that poison. No famous orator has ever been seen to come from Macedonia or from Persia.

What I have just said was prompted by my having talked with an Italian who served as chief steward to the late Cardinal Caraffa until his death. I got him to tell me

about his job. He harangued me on the art of feeding
with a professional gravity and demeanour as though
he were explaining some important point of Theology.
He listed differences of appetite: the appetite you have
when you are hungry, the one you have after the second
and third courses; what means there are of simply satis-
fying it or of sometimes exciting it and stimulating it;
how to govern the commonwealth of sauces, first in general then in particular, listing the qualities of every
ingredient and its effects; the different green-stuffs in their
season, the ones which must be served hot, the ones which
must be served cold as well as the ways of decorating
them and embellishing them to make them look even
more appetizing. After all that he embarked upon how
the service should be ordered, full of fine and weighty
considerations:

> *nec minimo sane discrimine refert*
> *Quo gestu lepores, et quo gallina secetur!*

[For it is of no small importance to know how to carve a hare or
a chicken!]

And all this was inflated with rich and magnificent words,
the very ones we use to discuss the government of an
empire. I was reminded of that man in the poem:

> *Hoc salsum est, hoc adustum est, hoc lautum est parum,*
> *Illud recte; iterum sic memento; sedulo*
> *Moneo quæ possum pro mea sapientia.*

*Postremo, tanquam in speculum, in patinas, Demea,*
*Inspicere jubeo, et moneo quid facto usus sit.*

['This is too salty; this has been burned; this needs to be properly washed; this is excellent – remember that next time.' I advise them carefully as far as my wisdom allows; finally I tell them, Demea, to polish the dishes until they can see their faces in them as in a mirror. I tell them the lot.]

Even the Greeks after all highly praised the order and arrangement which were observed in the banquet which Paulus Aemilius threw for them on his return from Macedonia; but I am not talking here of deeds but of words.

I cannot tell if others feel as I do, but when I hear our architects inflating their importance with big words such as pilasters, architraves, cornices, Corinthian style or Doric style, I cannot stop my thoughts from suddenly dwelling on the magic palaces of Apollidon: yet their deeds concern the wretched parts of my kitchen-door!

When you hear grammatical terms such as metonymy, metaphor and allegory do they not seem to refer to some rare, exotic tongue? Yet they are categories which apply to the chatter of your chambermaid.

It is a similar act of deception to use for our offices of state the same grandiloquent titles as the Romans did, even though they have no similarity of function and even less authority and power. Similar too – and a practice which will, in my judgement, bear witness one day to the singular ineptitude of our century – is our unworthily employing for anybody we like those glorious cognomens with which Antiquity honoured one or two great men every few hundred years. By universal acclaim Plato bore the name *divine*, and nobody thought to dispute it with him: now the Italians, who rightly boast of having in general more lively minds and saner discourse than other peoples of their time, have made a gift of it to Aretino, in whom (apart from a style of writing stuffed and simmering over with pointed sayings, ingenious it is true but fantastical and far-fetched, and apart from his eloquence – such as it is) I can see nothing beyond the common run of authors of his century, so far is he from even approaching that 'divinity' of the Ancients.

And the title Great we now attach to kings who have nothing beyond routine greatness.

## To philosophize is to learn how to die

*[ Montaigne comes to terms with his melancholy, now somewhat played down. He remains preoccupied with that fear of death – fear that is of the often excruciating act of dying – which in older times seems to have been widespread and acute. His treatment is rhetorical but not impersonal. Montaigne is on the way to discovering admirable qualities in common men and women.*

Cicero says that philosophizing is nothing other than getting ready to die. That is because study and contemplation draw our souls somewhat outside ourselves, keeping them occupied away from the body, a state which both resembles death and which forms a kind of apprenticeship for it; or perhaps it is because all the wisdom and argument in the world eventually come down to one conclusion; which is to teach us not to be afraid of dying.

In truth, either reason is joking or her target must be our happiness; all the labour of reason must be to make us live well, and at our ease, as Holy Scripture says. All the opinions in the world reach the same point, that pleasure is our target even though they may get there by different means; otherwise we would throw them out immediately, for who would listen to anyone whose goal was to achieve for us pain and suffering?

In this case the disagreements between the schools of philosophy are a matter of words. '*Transcurramus solertissimas nugas.*' [Let us skip quickly through those most frivolous trivialities.] More stubbornness and prickliness are there than is appropriate for so dedicated a vocation, but then, no matter what role a man may assume, he always plays his own part within it.

Even in virtue our ultimate aim – no matter what they say – is pleasure. I enjoy bashing people's ears with that word which runs so strongly counter to their minds. When pleasure is taken to mean the most profound delight and an exceeding happiness it is a better companion to virtue than anything else; and rightly so. Such pleasure is no less seriously pleasurable for being more lively, taut, robust and virile. We ought to have given virtue the more favourable, noble and natural name of pleasure not (as we have done) a name derived from *vis* (vigour).

There is that lower voluptuous pleasure which can only be said to have a disputed claim to the name not a privileged right to it. I find it less pure of lets and hindrances than virtue. Apart from having a savour which is fleeting, fluid and perishable, it has its vigils, fasts and travails, its blood and its sweat; it also has its own peculiar sufferings, which are sharp in so many different ways and accompanied by a satiety of such weight that it amounts to repentance.

Since we reckon that obstacles serve as a spur to that pleasure and as seasoning to its sweetness (on the grounds that in Nature contraries are enhanced by their contraries) we are quite wrong to say when we turn to virtue that identical obstacles and difficulties overwhelm her, making her austere and inaccessible, whereas (much more appropriately than for voluptuous pleasure) they ennoble, sharpen and enhance that holy, perfect pleasure which virtue procures for us. A man is quite unworthy of an acquaintance with virtue who weighs her fruit against the price she exacts; he knows neither her graces nor her ways. Those who proceed to teach us that the questing after virtue is rugged and wearisome whereas it is delightful to possess her can only mean that she always lacks delight. (For what human means have ever brought anyone to the joy of possessing her?) Even the most perfect of men have been satisfied with aspiring to her – not possessing her but drawing near to her. The contention is wrong, seeing that in every pleasure known to Man the very pursuit of it is pleasurable: the undertaking savours of the quality of the object it has in view; it effectively constitutes a large proportion of it and is consubstantial with it. There is a happiness and blessedness radiating from virtue; they fill all that appertains to her and every approach to her, from the first way in to the very last barrier.

Now one of virtue's main gifts is a contempt for death, which is the means of furnishing our life with easy tranquillity, of giving us a pure and friendly taste for it; without it every other pleasure is snuffed out. That is why all rules meet and concur in this one clause. It is true that they all lead us by common accord to despise pain, poverty and the other misfortunes to which human lives are subject, but they do not do so with the same care. That is partly because such misfortunes are not inevitable. (Most of Mankind spend their lives without tasting poverty; some without even experiencing pain or sickness, like Xenophilus the musician, who lived in good health to a hundred and six.) It is also because, if the worse comes to worse, we can sheer off the bung of our misfortunes whenever we like: death can end them. But, as for death itself, that is inevitable.

> *Omnes eodem cogimur, omnium*
> *Versatur urna, serius ocius*
> *Sors exitura et nos in æter-*
> *Num exitium impositura cymbæ.*

[All of our lots are shaken about in the Urn, destined sooner or later to be cast forth, placing us in everlasting exile via Charon's boat.]

And so if death makes us afraid, that is a subject of continual torment which nothing can assuage. There is no place where death cannot find us – even if we constantly twist our heads about in all directions as in a suspect land: '*Quae quasi saxum Tantalo semper impendet.*' [It is like the rock for ever hanging over the head of Tantalus.] Our assizes often send prisoners to be executed at the scene of their crimes. On the way there, take them past fair mansions and ply them with good cheer as much as you like –

> *. . . non Siculæ dapes*
> *Dulcem elaborabunt saporem,*
> *Non avium cytharæque cantus*
> *Somnum reducent –*

[even Sicilian banquets produce no sweet savours; not even the music of birdsong nor of lyre can bring back sleep] –

do you think they can enjoy it or that having the final purpose of their journey ever before their eyes will not spoil their taste for such entertainment?

> *Audit iter, numeratque dies, spacioque viarum*
> *Metitur vitam, torquetur peste futura*

[He inquires about the way; he counts the days; the length of his life is the length of those roads. He is tortured by future anguish.]

The end of our course is death. It is the objective necessarily within our sights. If death frightens us how can we go one step forward without anguish? For ordinary people the remedy is not to think about it; but what brutish insensitivity can produce so gross a blindness? They lead the donkey by the tail:

*Qui capite ipse suo instituit vestigia retro.*

[They walk forward with their heads turned backwards.]

No wonder that they often get caught in a trap. You can frighten such people simply by mentioning death (most of them cross themselves as when the Devil is named); and since it is mentioned in wills, never expect them to draw one up before the doctor has pronounced the death-sentence. And then, in the midst of pain and terror, God only knows what shape their good judgement kneads it into!

(That syllable 'death' struck Roman ears too roughly; the very word was thought to bring ill-luck, so they learned to soften and dilute it with periphrases. Instead of saying *He is dead* they said *He has ceased to live* or *He has lived*. They found consolation in living, even in a past tense! Whence our 'late' (*feu*) So-and-So: 'he was' So-and-So.)

Perhaps it is a case of, 'Repayment delayed means money in hand', as they say; I was born between eleven and noon on the last day of February, one thousand five hundred and thirty-three (as we date things nowadays, beginning the year in January); it is exactly a fortnight since I became thirty-nine: 'I ought to live at least as long again; meanwhile it would be mad to think of something

so far off'. – Yes, but all leave life in the same circum-
stances, young and old alike. Everybody goes out as
though he had just come in. Moreover, however decrepit
a man may be, he thinks he still has another twenty years
to go in the body, so long as he has Methuselah ahead of
him. Silly fool, you! Where your life is concerned, who
has decided the term? You are relying on doctors' tales;
look at facts and experience instead. As things usually
go, you have been living for some time now by favour
extraordinary. You have already exceeded the usual term
of life; to prove it, just count how many more of your
acquaintances have died younger than you are compared
with those who have reached your age. Just make a list
of people who have ennobled their lives by fame: I wager
that we shall find more who died before thirty-five than
after. It is full of reason and piety to take as our example
the manhood of Jesus Christ: his life ended at thirty-three.
The same term applies to Alexander, the greatest man
who was simply man.

Death can surprise us in so many ways:

> *Quid quisque vitet, nunquam homini satis*
> *Cautum est in horas.*

[No man knows what dangers he should avoid from one hour to
another.]

Leaving aside fevers and pleurisies, who would ever have
thought that a Duke of Brittany was to be crushed to

death in a crowd, as one was during the state entry into Lyons of Pope Clement, who came from my part of the world! Have you not seen one of our kings killed at sport? And was not one of his ancestors killed by a bump from a pig? Aeschylus was warned against a falling house; he was always on the alert, but in vain: he was killed by the shell of a tortoise which slipped from the talons of an eagle in flight. Another choked to death on a pip from a grape; an Emperor died from a scratch when combing his hair; Aemilius Lepidus, from knocking his foot on his own doorstep; Aufidius from bumping into a door of his Council chamber. Those who died between a woman's thighs include Cornelius Gallus, a praetor; Tigillinus, a captain of the Roman Guard; Ludovico, the son of Guy di Gonzaga, the Marquis of Mantua; and – providing even worse examples – Speucippus the Platonic philosopher, and one of our Popes.

Then there was that wretched judge Bebius; he was just granting a week's extra time to a litigant when he died of a seizure: his own time had run out. Caius Julius, a doctor, was putting ointment on the eyes of a patient when death closed his. And if I may include a personal example, Captain Saint-Martin, my brother, died at the age of twenty-three while playing tennis; he was felled by a blow from a tennis-ball just above the right ear. There was no sign of bruising or of a wound. He did not even sit down or take a rest; yet five or six hours later he was dead from an apoplexy caused by that blow.

When there pass before our eyes examples such as these, so frequent and so ordinary, how can we ever rid ourselves of thoughts of death or stop imagining that death has us by the scruff of the neck at every moment?

You might say: 'But what does it matter how you do it, so long as you avoid pain?' I agree with that. If there were any way at all of sheltering from Death's blows – even by crawling under the skin of a calf – I am not the man to recoil from it. It is enough for me to spend my time contentedly. I deal myself the best hand I can, and then accept it. It can be as inglorious or as unexemplary as you please:

> *prætulerim delirus inersque videri,*
> *Dum mea delectent mala me, vel denique fallant,*
> *Quam sapere et ringi.*

[I would rather be delirious or a dullard if my faults pleased me, or at least deceived me, rather than to be wise and snarling.]

But it is madness to think you can succeed that way. They come and they go and they trot and they dance: and never a word about death. All well and good. Yet when death does come – to them, their wives, their children, their friends – catching them unawares and unprepared, then what storms of passion overwhelm them, what cries, what fury, what despair! Have you ever seen anything brought so low, anything so changed, so confused?

We must start providing for it earlier. Even if such brutish indifference could find lodgings in the head of an intelligent man (which seems quite impossible to me) it sells its wares too dearly. If death were an enemy which could be avoided I would counsel borrowing the arms of cowardice. But it cannot be done. Death can catch you just as easily as a coward on the run or as an honourable man:

> *Nempe et fugacem persequitur virum,*
> *Nec parcit imbellis juventæ*
> *Poplitibus, timidoque tergo;*

[It hounds the man who runs away, and it does not spare the legs fearful backs of unwarlike youth;]

no tempered steel can protect your shoulders;

> *Ille licet ferro cautus se condat ære,*
> *Mors tamen inclusum protrahet inde caput;*

[No use a man hiding prudently behind iron or brass: Death will know how to make him stick out his cowering head;]

we must learn to stand firm and to fight it.

To begin depriving death of its greatest advantage over us, let us adopt a way clean contrary to that common one; let us deprive death of its strangeness; let us frequent it, let us get used to it; let us have nothing more often in mind than death. At every instant let us evoke it in our imagination under all its aspects. Whenever a horse stumbles, a tile falls or a pin pricks however slightly, let us at once chew over this thought: 'Supposing that was death itself?' With that, let us brace ourselves and make an effort. In the midst of joy and feasting let our refrain be one which recalls our human condition. Let us never be carried away by pleasure so strongly that we fail to recall occasionally how many are the ways in which that joy of ours is subject to death or how many are the fashions in which death threatens to snatch it away. That is what the Egyptians did: in the midst of all their banquets and good cheer they would bring in a mummified corpse to serve as a warning to the guests:

> *Omnem crede diem tibi diluxisse supremum.*
> *Grata superveniet, quæ non sperabitur hora.*

[Believe that each day was the last to shine on you. If it comes, any unexpected hour will be welcome indeed.]

We do not know where death awaits us: so let us wait for it everywhere. To practise death is to practise freedom. A man who has learned how to die has unlearned how to be a slave. Knowing how to die gives us freedom from subjection and constraint. Life has no evil for him who has thoroughly understood that loss of life is not an evil. Paulus Aemilius was sent a messenger by that wretched King of Macedonia who was his prisoner, begging not to be led in his triumphant procession. He replied: 'Let him beg that favour from himself.'

It is true that, in all things, if Nature does not lend a hand art and industry do not progress very far. I myself am not so much melancholic as an idle dreamer: from the outset there was no topic I ever concerned myself with more than with thoughts about death – even in the most licentious period of my life.

*Jucundum cum aetas florida ver ageret.*

[When my blossoming youth rejoiced in spring.]

Among the games and the courting many thought I was standing apart chewing over some jealousy or the uncertainty of my aspirations: meanwhile I was reflecting on someone or other who, on leaving festivities just like these, had been surprised by a burning fever and his end, with his head full of idleness, love and merriment – just like me; and the same could be dogging me now:

*Jam fuerit, nec post unquam revocare licebit.*

[The present will soon be the past, never to be recalled.]

Thoughts such as these did not furrow my brow any more than others did. At first it does seem impossible not to feel the sting of such ideas, but if you keep handling them and running through them you eventually tame them. No doubt about that. Otherwise I would, for my part, be in continual terror and frenzy: for no man ever had less confidence than I did that he would go on living;

and no man ever counted less on his life proving long. Up till now I have enjoyed robust good health almost uninterruptedly: yet that never extends my hopes for life any more than sickness shortens them. Every moment it seems to me that I am running away from myself. And I ceaselessly chant the refrain, 'Anything you can do another day can be done now.'

In truth risks and dangers do little or nothing to bring us nearer to death. If we think of all the millions of threats which remain hanging over us, apart from the one which happens to appear most menacing just now, we shall real-ize that death is equally near when we are vigorous or feverish, at sea or at home, in battle or in repose. '*Nemo altero fragilior est: nemo in crastinam sui certior.*' [No man is frailer than another: no man more certain of the morrow.]

If I have only one hour's work to do before I die, I am never sure I have time enough to finish it. The other day someone was going through my notebooks and found a declaration about something I wanted done after my death. I told him straight that, though I was hale and healthy and but a league away from my house, I had hastened to jot it down because I had not been absolutely certain of getting back home. Being a man who broods over his thoughts and stores them up inside him, I am always just about as ready as I can be: when death does suddenly appear, it will bear no new warning for me. As far as we possibly can we must always have our boots on, ready to go; above all we should take care to have no outstanding business with anyone else.

> *Quid brevi fortes jaculamur ævo*
> *Multa?*

[Why, in so brief a span do we find strength to make so many projects?]

We shall have enough to do then without adding to it.

One man complains less of death itself than of its cutting short the course of a fine victory; another, that he has to depart before marrying off his daughter or arranging the education of his children; one laments the company of his wife; another, of his son; as though they were the principal attributes of his being.

I am now ready to leave, thank God, whenever He pleases, regretting nothing except life itself – if its loss should happen to weigh heavy on me. I am untying all the knots. I have already half-said my adieus to everyone but myself. No man has ever prepared to leave the world more simply nor more fully than I have. No one has more completely let go of everything than I try to do.

> *Miser o miser, aiunt, omnia ademit*
> *Una dies infesta mihi tot præmia vitæ.*

['I am wretched, so wretched,' they say: 'One dreadful day has stripped me of all life's rewards.']

And the builder says:

*Michel de Montaigne*

> *Manent opera interrupta, minaeque*
> *Murorum ingentes.*

[My work remains unfinished; huge walls may fall down.]

We ought not to plan anything on so large a scale – at least, not if we are to get all worked up if we cannot see it through to the end.

We are born for action:

> *Cum moriar, medium solvare inter opus.*

[When I die, may I be in the midst of my work.]

I want us to be doing things, prolonging life's duties as much as we can; I want Death to find me planting my cabbages, neither worrying about it nor the unfinished gardening. I once saw a man die who, right to the last, kept lamenting that destiny had cut the thread of the history he was writing when he had only got up to our fifteenth or sixteenth king!

> *Illud in his rebus non addunt, nec tibi earum*
> *Jam desiderium rerum super insidet una!*

[They never add, that desire for such things does not linger on in your remains!]

We must throw off such humours; they are harmful and vulgar.

Our graveyards have been planted next to churches, says Lycurgus, so that women, children and lesser folk should grow accustomed to seeing a dead man without feeling terror, and so that this continual spectacle of bones, tombs and funerals should remind us of our human condition:

> *Quin etiam exhilarare viris convivia cœde*
> *Mos olim, et miscere epulis spectacula dira*
> *Certantum ferro, sœpe et super ipsa cadentum*
> *Pocula respersis non parco sanguine mensis;*

[It was once the custom, moreover, to enliven feasts with human slaughter and to entertain guests with the cruel sight of gladiators fighting: they often fell among the goblets, flooding the tables with their blood;]

so too, after their festivities the Egyptians used to display before their guests a huge portrait of death, held up by a man crying, 'Drink and be merry: once dead you will look like this'; similarly, I have adopted the practice of always having death not only in my mind but on my lips. There is nothing I inquire about more readily than how men have died: what did they say? How did they look? What expression did they have? There are no passages in the history books which I note more attentively. That I have a particular liking for such matters is shown by the examples with which I stuff my book. If I were a scribbler I would produce a compendium with commentaries of the various ways men have died. (Anyone who taught men how to die would teach them how to live.) Dicearchus did write a book with some such title, but for another and less useful purpose.

People will tell me that the reality of death so far exceeds the thought that when we actually get there all our fine fencing amounts to nothing. Let them say so: there is no doubt whatsoever that meditating on it beforehand confers great advantages. Anyway, is it nothing to get even that far without faltering or feverish agitation?

But there is more to it than that: Nature herself lends us a hand and gives us courage. If our death is violent and short we have no time to feel afraid: if it be otherwise, I have noticed that as an illness gets more and more hold on me I naturally slip into a kind of contempt for life. I find that a determination to die is harder to digest when I am in good health than when I am feverish, especially since I no longer hold so firmly to the pleasures of life once I begin to lose the use and enjoyment of them, and can look on death with a far less terrified gaze. That leads me to hope that the further I get from good health and the nearer I approach to death the more easily I will come to terms with exchanging one for the other. Just as I have in several other matters assayed the truth of Caesar's assertion that things often look bigger from afar than close to, I have also found that I was much more terrified of illness when I was well than when I felt ill. Being in a happy state, all pleasure and vigour, leads me to get the other state quite out of proportion, so that I mentally increase all its discomforts by half and imagine them heavier than they prove to be when I have to bear them.

I hope that the same will apply to me when I die. It is normal to experience change and decay: let us note how Nature robs us of our sense of loss and decline. What does an old man still retain of his youthful vigour and of his own past life?

*Heu senibus vitae portio quanta manet.*

[Alas, what little of life's portion remains with the aged.]

When a soldier of Caesar's guard, broken and worn out, came up to him in the street and begged leave to kill himself, Caesar looked at his decrepit bearing and said with a smile: 'So you think you are still alive, then?'

If any of us were to be plunged into old age all of a sudden I do not think that the change would be bearable. But, almost imperceptibly, Nature leads us by the hand down a gentle slope; little by little, step by step, she engulfs us in that pitiful state and breaks us in, so that we feel no jolt when youth dies in us, although in essence and in truth that is a harsher death than the total extinction of a languishing life as old age dies. For it is not so grievous a leap from a wretched existence to non-existence as it is from a sweet existence in full bloom to one full of travail and pain.

When our bodies are bent and stooping low they have less strength for supporting burdens. So too for our souls:

45

we must therefore educate and train them for their encounter with that adversary, death; for the soul can find no rest while she remains afraid of him. But once she does find assurance she can boast that it is impossible for anxiety, anguish, fear or even the slightest dissatisfaction to dwell within her. And that almost surpasses our human condition.

> *Non vultus instantis tyranni*
> *Mente quatit solida, neque Auster*
> *Dux inquieti turbidus Adriæ,*
> *Nec fulminantis magna Jovis manus.*

[Nothing can shake such firmness: neither the threatening face of a tyrant, nor the South Wind (that tempestuous Master of the Stormy Adriatic) nor even the mighty hand of thundering Jove.]

She has made herself Mistress of her passions and her lusts, Mistress of destitution, shame, poverty and of all other injuries of Fortune. Let any of us who can gain such a superiority do so: for here is that true and sovereign freedom which enables us to cock a snook at force and injustice and to laugh at manacles and prisons:

> *in manicis, et*
> *Compedibus, sævo te sub custode tenebo.*
> *Ipse Deus simul atque volam, me solvet: opinor,*
> *Hoc sentit, moriar. Mors ultima linea rerum est.*

['I will shackle your hands and feet and keep you under a cruel gaoler.' – 'God himself will set me free as soon as I ask him to.' (He means, I think, 'I will die': for death is the last line of all.)]

Our religion has never had a surer human foundation than contempt for life; rational argument (though not it alone) summons us to such contempt: for why should we fear to lose something which, once lost, cannot be regretted? And since we are threatened by so many kinds of death is it not worse to fear them all than to bear one? Death is inevitable: does it matter when it comes? When Socrates was told that the Thirty Tyrants had condemned him to death, he retorted, 'And nature, them!'

How absurd to anguish over our passing into freedom from all anguish. Just as our birth was the birth of all things for us, so our death will be the death of them all. That is why it is equally mad to weep because we shall not be alive a hundred years from now and to weep because we were not alive a hundred years ago. Death is the origin of another life. We wept like this and it cost us just as dear when we entered into this life, similarly stripping off our former veil as we did so. Nothing can be grievous which occurs but once; is it reasonable to fear for so long a time something which lasts so short a time? Living a long life or a short life are made all one by death: *long* and *short* do not apply to that which is no more. Aristotle says that there are tiny creatures on the river Hypanis whose life lasts one

47

single day: those which die at eight in the morning die in youth; those which die at five in the evening die of senility. Which of us would not laugh if so momentary a span counted as happiness or unhappiness? Yet if we compare our own span against eternity or even against the span of mountains, rivers, stars, trees or, indeed, of some animals, then saying *shorter* or *longer* becomes equally ridiculous.

Nature drives us that way, too: 'Leave this world,' she says, 'just as you entered it. That same journey from death to life, which you once made without suffering or fear, make it again from life to death. Your death is a part of the order of the universe; it is a part of the life of the world:

> *inter se mortales mutua vivunt . . .*
> *Et quasi cursores vitaï lampada tradunt.*

[Mortal creatures live lives dependent on each other; like runners in a relay they pass on the torch of life.]

Shall I change, just for you, this beautiful interwoven structure! Death is one of the attributes you were created with; death is a part of you; you are running away from yourself; this *being* which you enjoy is equally divided between death and life. From the day you were born your path leads to death as well as life:

> *Prima, quae vitam dedit, hora, carpsit.*

[Our first hour gave us life and began to devour it.]

> *Nascentes morimur, finisque ab origine pendet.*

[As we are born we die; the end of our life is attached to its beginning.]

All that you live, you have stolen from life; you live at her expense. Your life's continual task is to build your death. You are *in* death while you are *in* life: when you are no more *in* life you are after death. Or if you prefer it thus: after life you are dead, but during life you are dying: and death touches the dying more harshly than the dead, in more lively a fashion and more essentially.

'If you have profited from life, you have had your fill; go away satisfied:

> *Cur non ut plenus vitae conviva recedis?*

[Why not withdraw from life like a guest replete?]

But if you have never learned how to use life, if life is useless to you, what does it matter if you have lost it? What do you still want it for?

> *Cur amplius addere quæris*
> *Rursum quod pereat male, et ingratum occidat omne?*

[Why seek to add more, just to lose it again, wretchedly, without joy?]

Life itself is neither a good nor an evil: life is where good or evil find a place, depending on how you make it for them.

'If you have lived one day, you have seen everything.

One day equals all days. There is no other light, no other night. The Sun, Moon and Stars, disposed just as they are now, were enjoyed by your grandsires and will entertain your great-grandchildren:

> *Non alium videre patres: aliumve nepotes*
> *Aspicient.*

[Your fathers saw none other: none other shall your progeny discern.]

And at the worst estimate the division and variety of all the acts of my play are complete in one year. If you have observed the vicissitude of my four seasons you know they embrace the childhood, youth, manhood and old age of the World. Its play is done. It knows no other trick but to start all over again. Always it will be the same.

> *Versamur ibidem, atque insumus usque;*

[We turn in the same circle, for ever;]

> *Atque in se sua per vestigia volvitur annus.*

[And the year rolls on again through its own traces.]

I have not the slightest intention of creating new pastimes for you.

> *Nam tibi præterea quod machiner, inveniamque*
> *Quod placeat, nihil est, eadem sunt omnia semper.*

[For there is nothing else I can make or discover to please you: all things are the same for ever.]

Make way for others as others did for you. The first part of equity is equality. Who can complain of being included when all are included?

'It is no good going on living: it will in no wise shorten the time you will stay dead. It is all for nothing: you will be just as long in that state which you fear as though you had died at the breast;

> *licet, quod vis, vivendo vincere secla,*
> *Mors æterna tamen nihilominus illa manebit.*

[Triumph over time and live as long as you please: death eternal will still be waiting for you.]

'And yet I shall arrange that you have no unhappiness:

> *In vera nescis nullum fore morte alium te,*
> *Qui possit vivus tibi te lugere peremptum,*
> *Stansque jacentem.*

[Do you not know that in real death there will be no second You, living to lament your death and standing by your corpse.]

"You" will not desire the life which now you so much lament.

> *Nec sibi enim quisquam tum se vitamque requirit . . .*
> *Nec desiderium nostri nos afficit ullum.*

[Then no one worries about his life or his self; . . . we feel no yearning for our own being.]

Death is less to be feared than nothing – if there be anything less than nothing:

> *multo mortem minus ad nos esse putandum*
> *Si minus esse potest quam quod nihil esse videmus.*

[We should think death to be less – if anything is 'less' than what we can see to be nothing at all.]

'Death does not concern you, dead or alive; alive, because you are: dead, because you are no more.

'No one dies before his time; the time you leave behind you is no more yours than the time which passed before you were born; and does not concern you either:

> *Respice enim quam nil ad nos ante acta vetustas*
> *Temporis æterní fuerit.*

[Look back and see that the aeons of eternity before we were born have been nothing to us.]

'Wherever your life ends, there all of it ends. The usefulness of living lies not in duration but in what you make of it. Some have lived long and lived little. See to it while you are still here. Whether you have lived enough depends not on a count of years but on your will.

'Do you think you will never arrive whither you are ceaselessly heading? Yet every road has its end. And, if it is a relief to have company, is not the whole world proceeding at the same pace as you are?

*Omnia te vita perfuncta sequentur.*

[All things will follow you when their life is done.]

Does not everything move with the same motion as you do? Is there anything which is not growing old with you? At this same instant that you die hundreds of men, of beasts and of other creatures are dying too.

*Nam nox nulla diem, neque noctem aurora sequuta est,*
*Qua non audierit mistos vagitibus ægris*
*Ploratus, mortis comites et funeris atri.*

[No night has ever followed day, no dawn has ever followed night, without hearing, interspersed among the wails of infants, the cries of pain attending death and sombre funerals.]

'Why do you pull back when retreat is impossible? You have seen cases enough where men were lucky to die, avoiding great misfortunes by doing so: but have you ever seen anyone for whom death turned out badly? And it is very simple-minded of you to condemn something which you have never experienced either yourself or through another. Why do you complain of me or of Destiny? Do we do you wrong? Should you govern us or should we govern you? You may not have finished your stint but you have finished your life. A small man is no less whole than a tall one. Neither men nor their lives are measured by the yard. Chiron refused immortality when he was told of its characteristics by his father Saturn, the god of time and of duration.

'Truly imagine how much less bearable for Man, and how much more painful, would be a life which lasted for ever rather than the life which I have given you. If you did not have death you would curse me, for ever, for depriving you of it.

'Seeing what advantages death holds I have deliberately mixed a little anguish into it to stop you from embracing it too avidly or too injudiciously. To lodge you in that moderation which I require of you, neither fleeing from life nor yet fleeing from death, I have tempered them both between the bitter and the sweet.

'I taught Thales, the foremost of your Sages, that living and dying are things indifferent. So, when asked "why he did not go and die then," he very wisely replied: "Because it *is* indifferent."

'Water, Earth, Air and Fire and the other parts of this my edifice are no more instrumental to your life than to your death. Why are you afraid of your last day? It brings you no closer to your death than any other did. The last step does not make you tired: it shows that you are tired. All days lead to death: the last one gets there.'

Those are the good counsels of Nature, our Mother.

I have often wondered why the face of death, seen in ourselves or in other men, appears incomparably less terrifying to us in war than in our own homes – otherwise armies would consist of doctors and cry-babies – and why, since death is ever the same, there is always more stead-fastness among village-folk and the lower orders than among all the rest. I truly believe that what frightens us more than death itself are those terrifying grimaces and preparations with which we surround it – a brand new way of life: mothers, wives and children weeping; visits from people stunned and beside themselves with grief; the presence of a crowd of servants, pale and tear-stained; a bedchamber without daylight; candles lighted; our bedside besieged by doctors and preachers; in short, all about us is horror and terror. We are under the ground, buried in our graves already! Children are frightened of their very friends when they see them masked. So are we. We must rip the masks off things as well as off people. Once we have done that we shall find underneath only that same death which a valet and a chambermaid got through recently, without being afraid. Blessed the death which leaves no time for preparing such gatherings of mourners.